MEMORABLE
ROASTS
TRADITIONAL FARE

D0725001

KÖNEMANN

BEEF AND VEAL

Beef Rib Eye Roast with Gravy

The tradition of a beef or veal roast seems to signify a special meal. Beef and veal roasts combine beautifully with the full-bodied flavors of red wine, gravy, garlic, mustard and pungent horseradish. Suitable cuts for roasting include beef rib, rib eye, eye round, round tip, bottom round, rump, tenderloin, chuck eye, top loin, top round and tri-tip (bottom sirloin). Veal roasts include the rib, crown, blade, arm, shoulder, rump, breast, loin and sirloin.

COOKING TIMES
Place roast, fat side up, on a rack in a roasting pan. Insert meat thermometer into thickest part, not touching bone or fat. Do not add water and do not cover. Roast until meat thermometer registers 5° to 10°F below desired doneness. During standing, the roast continues to rise 5° to 10°F. Allow roast to stand 15 to 20 minutes before serving.
Recommended internal temperatures
Rare: 140°F
Medium-rare: 150°F
Medium: 160°F
Well-done: 170°F
Ground beef: 160°F
Visual guide to determining doneness
Rare: center is bright red; pinkish toward outer portion.
Medium: center is light pink; outer portion is brown.
Well-done: uniform brown throughout.
Note: Ground beef should be cooked to 160°F, until no longer pink and juices run clear.

Beef Rib Eye Roast with Gravy

Preparation time:
  10 minutes
Cooking time:
  1 hour and 20 minutes
Serves 12

1 beef rib eye roast
  (about 4 pounds)
pepper
1 clove garlic, crushed
Gravy
2 tablespoons
  all-purpose flour
1¾ cups beef stock
¼ cup red wine
salt and pepper

1 Rub outside of meat with pepper and garlic. Place roast, fat side up, on rack in a shallow roasting pan. Insert meat thermometer.
2 Roast in a moderate 350°F oven, allowing 18–20 minutes per pound for rare, 20–22 minutes per pound for medium. Remove roast from oven when meat thermometer registers 135°F for rare or 155°F for medium. Cover loosely with foil. Let stand 15–20 minutes before carving.
3 To prepare Gravy: Drain off all except 2 tablespoons of fat from roasting pan. Place pan over a low heat. Add flour. Stir well. Cook, stirring constantly, over medium heat until well browned, taking care not to burn.
4 Combine beef stock and wine. Gradually stir into flour mixture. Cook and stir until thickened. Cook and stir 1 minute more. Season.
5 Serve beef with gravy, Yorkshire Puddings, roasted potatoes and creamed brussels sprouts, if desired.

HINT
If serving Beef Rib Eye Roast with Yorkshire Puddings you will need to keep the beef in a warm spot while the oven is hot for baking the puddings. If serving roast potatoes, crisp them in the hot oven while baking the puddings.

How to Carve a Rib Roast

1 Remove upper spinal bones. Try not to pierce the meat. Steady meat with the back of a carving fork. Separate meat from bone by cutting horizontally along contours of rib.

2 Slice the beef vertically. Each slice will fall free as you cut.

Standing Rib Roast with Pâté

Preparation time:
 30 minutes
Cooking time:
 2–3 hours
Serves 6–8

1 *slice bacon, chopped*
1 *small onion, finely*
 chopped
4 *ounces mushrooms,*
 finely chopped
4 *ounces purchased pâté*
½ *cup fine dry bread*
 crumbs
2 *tablespoons chopped*
 fresh parsley
½ *teaspoon dried mixed*
 herbs
freshly ground black
 pepper to taste
1 *egg, lightly beaten*

1 *6–8 pound beef rib*
 roast (see note)

1 Place bacon in a dry skillet. Heat gently until beginning to soften. Add onion and mushrooms. Cook, stirring, for 5 minutes or until tender. Transfer to a bowl. Mix in pâté, bread crumbs, parsley, herbs, pepper and egg.

2 Cut a slit in the meat between rib bones and outer layer of fat at the narrow end. Remove any excess fat.

3 Fill cavity with pâté mixture. Replace flap. Secure with a skewer, if necessary.

4 Place meat, fat side up, on rack in a shallow roasting pan. Roast in a 325°F oven until desired doneness, allowing 23–25 minutes per pound for rare, 27–30 minutes per pound for medium. Remove roast from oven when meat thermometer registers 135°F for rare or 155°F for medium.

5 Allow to rest for 15–20 minutes before carving. Serve with gravy, roast potatoes and vegetables.

Note: Ask your butcher to help prepare your roast by sawing through the upper spinal bones so that they will be easy to remove before carving (see How to Carve a Rib Roast).

Standing Rib Roast with Pâté

Beef with Blue Cheese in Pastry

Preparation time:
 45 minutes
Cooking time:
 30 minutes
Serves 8

1 *pound fresh spinach
 or 1 10-ounce
 package frozen
 spinach*
¼ *cup butter or
 margarine*
1 *3-pound beef
 tenderloin roast,
 trimmed*
2 *sheets frozen puff
 pastry, thawed*
6 *ounces blue cheese,
 softened*
1 *sheet puff pastry extra
 (optional)*
1 *egg, lightly beaten*

1 To prepare spinach: Remove stalk from leaves by cutting along both sides of stalk through center of each leaf. Wash leaves well. If using frozen spinach, allow to thaw. Squeeze out excess water.
2 Drop fresh spinach leaves into boiling water. Cook for 30 seconds or until leaves are just softened. Drain. Refresh in cold water. Pat dry with paper towels.
3 Heat butter in a large skillet. Add meat. Brown on all sides to seal in juices. Cool. Reserve pan juices.

4 Place pastry on a flat surface. Overlap edges by ½ inch. Seal by pressing together well. Arrange spinach over pastry leaving a 2-inch border.
5 Spread or crumble cheese over spinach. Place beef in center of pastry. Fold in narrow ends. Fold remaining pastry over to enclose beef. Turn seam to underside. Decorate with extra pastry, if desired. Brush with egg.
6 Place in a lightly greased shallow baking pan. Roast in a 425°F oven for 25–30 minutes or until pastry is golden. Rest, covered with foil, for 10 minutes.

HINT
Pieces of meat are often 'seared' before roasting by browning quickly in hot butter or oil to seal in juices and to give a tender result.

Beef with Blue Cheese in Pastry

Peppered Beef with Béarnaise Sauce

Peppered Beef with Béarnaise Sauce

Preparation time:
45 minutes
Cooking time:
50–70 minutes
Serves 8

1 3-pound beef eye
  round roast
1 tablespoon oil
2 cloves garlic, crushed
1 tablespoon crushed
  black peppercorns
2 teaspoons crushed
  coriander seeds or
  ground coriander
Béarnaise Sauce
½ cup butter, at room
  temperature
3 shallots, chopped
¼ cup dry white wine
2 tablespoons tarragon
  vinegar
4 egg yolks
1 tablespoon chopped
  fresh tarragon

1 Trim meat of excess fat. Brush with oil and garlic. Roll meat in combined peppercorns and coriander seeds.
2 Place meat on a rack in a shallow roasting pan. Roast in a 325°F oven, allowing 20–22 minutes per pound or until meat thermometer registers 135°F. Cover loosely with foil. Let stand 15–20 minutes before carving.
3 Meanwhile, prepare Béarnaise Sauce. Cut butter into thirds.
4 Place shallots, wine and vinegar in a small pan. Cook rapidly until about 2 tablespoons of the liquid is left.
5 In the top of a double boiler combine egg yolks and shallot mixture. Place over simmering water. Add one piece of butter. Cook, stirring rapidly, until butter melts and sauce begins to thicken. Add remaining butter, one piece at a time, stirring constantly. Cook and stir 1–2 minutes until thickened. Stir in fresh tarragon. Immediately remove from heat. If sauce is too thick or curdles, immediately beat in 1–2 tablespoons hot water.
6 Slice meat and serve with sauce.

HINT
The easiest way to test if a roast is done is by feel. Give the center of the meat a quick pinch—the more yielding it is, the rarer the meat will be.

Veal Roast with Peppercorn Sauce

Preparation time:
  30 minutes
Cooking time:
  1 hour and 45 minutes
Serves 9

1 3-pound boneless veal
  rump roast
2 tablespoons Dijon
  mustard
freshly ground pepper
¼ cup chicken broth
¼ cup dry white wine
½ teaspoon fines herbs
2 tablespoons brandy
¼ cup heavy cream
1 tablespoon bottled
  green peppercorns,
  drained

1 Place roast, fat side up, on a rack in a shallow roasting pan. Spread mustard evenly over roast. Sprinkle with pepper.
2 Insert meat thermometer so bulb is centered in thickest part and not touching fat. Do not add water. Do not cover.
3 Roast in a 325°F oven until a meat thermometer registers 155°F, approximately 33–35 minutes per pound. Transfer veal to serving platter; remove string. Cover and keep warm.
4 Add meat juices to a small saucepan. Add chicken broth, wine and herbs. Bring to a boil; reduce heat and simmer uncovered until reduced. Stir in brandy, cream and crushed green peppercorns. Do not boil.
5 Thinly slice veal and serve with sauce.

Herbed Roast Beef with Sauce Bordelaise

Preparation time:
  30 minutes
Cooking time:
  1–1¼ hours
Serves 6

1 2-pound tri-tip
  (bottom sirloin) roast
freshly ground black
  pepper
1 teaspoon dried thyme,
  crushed
1 teaspoon dried
  oregano, crushed
1 clove garlic, peeled
Sauce Bordelaise
1¼ cups beef stock
1 cup dry red wine
¼ cup tomato paste
2 tablespoons butter
2 bay leaves
2 teaspoons all-purpose
  flour

1 Rub outside of meat with plenty of black pepper, thyme, oregano and garlic clove. Place on a rack in a shallow roasting pan.
2 Roast in a moderate 425°F oven, allowing 30–40 minutes per pound or until meat thermometer registers 135°F. Cover loosely with foil. Let stand for 15–20 minutes before carving.
3 To prepare Sauce Bordelaise: Combine stock, wine, tomato paste, butter and bay leaves in medium saucepan. Bring to a boil. Reduce heat and simmer, uncovered, until reduced by half. Remove bay leaves.
4 Drain off all but 1 tablespoon of fat from roasting pan. Place pan over medium heat. Add flour and stir well to incorporate all the brown bits. Stir constantly until well browned. Gradually stir in stock and wine mixture. Stir constantly until sauce boils and thickens. Slice beef and serve with sauce.

HINT
Roast meats all benefit from a short rest in a warm place before carving, keeping the juices within the meat and making it easier to carve.

Herbed Roast Beef with Sauce Bordelaise

Rack of Veal with Herbed Crust

Preparation time:
  30 minutes
Cooking time:
  1–1½ hours
Serves 6

1 3-pound rack of veal
  or lamb (6 cutlets)
1 cup fresh bread crumbs
½ cup fine dry bread
  crumbs
1 tablespoon finely
  chopped parsley
1 tablespoon finely
  chopped basil
2 egg whites, lightly
  beaten
2 cloves garlic, crushed
1 tablespoon oil
2 tablespoons butter,
  melted
Lemon Sauce
¼ cup dry white wine
¼ cup water
2 tablespoons lemon juice
1 teaspoon sugar
⅓ cup butter, cubed
2 teaspoons finely
  chopped parsley

1 Trim any excess fat
from veal. Combine
fresh and dry bread
crumbs, parsley and
basil. Add combined egg
whites, garlic, oil and
butter. Mix well. Add a
little water if mixture is
too dry.
2 Press mixture firmly
over fatty side of rack.
Place rack, crust side up,
in a shallow roasting
pan. Roast in a 325°F
oven for 1–1½ hours.
3 Allow meat to stand
in a warm place for
10–15 minutes before
slicing. Drain off all
except 2 tablespoons of
cooking juices in
roasting pan.
4 To prepare Lemon
Sauce: Heat roasting pan
on top of stove. Add
wine, water, lemon juice
and sugar. Bring to a
boil; reduce heat. Simmer
uncovered until reduced
to ½ cup of liquid.
5 Whisk in butter, one
cube at a time. Add
parsley. Cut veal or lamb
into cutlets. Serve lemon
sauce over each cutlet.

Note: Ask your butcher
to cut through bones for
ease of slicing.

HINT
Veal has a relatively
delicate and mild meat
flavor. It should have
a smooth, firm texture
when it is cooked.
The following
seasonings go nicely
with veal: sage,
marjoram, rosemary,
oregano, black
pepper, cinnamon,
garlic and mustard.

Rack of Veal with Herbed Crust

LAMB

Roast Lamb with Orange and Rosemary Stuffing, Wine Gravy, Braised Onions in Cream and Broccoli with Browned Nut Butter Sauce

Spring is the time to enjoy tender succulent lamb; we boast some of the best in the world. Our recipes reflect the versatility of this meat by incorporating flavors from other lands to complement its distinctive taste.

The flavor of lamb roast is enhanced by the addition of garlic, rosemary, oregano, mint and lemon.

Suitable cuts for roasting include leg, sirloin roast, shoulder, rib roast, crown roast and rack of lamb.

Roast Lamb with Orange and Rosemary Stuffing

Preparation time:
 50 minutes
Cooking time:
 1½–2 hours
Serves 8

1 7-pound leg of lamb, boned
2 cups fresh bread crumbs
2 tablespoons finely chopped rosemary
¼ cup coarsely chopped pecans
2 tablespoons orange marmalade
1 tablespoon grated orange peel
2 tablespoons orange juice
1 tablespoon orange marmalade, extra
½ cup dry white wine
1 teaspoon grated orange peel, extra
2 tablespoons orange marmalade, extra

1 Trim excess fat from lamb; lay open on a flat surface. Combine bread crumbs, rosemary and pecans. Add combined marmalade, orange peel and juice. Mix lightly, adding extra orange juice if necessary to bind.
2 Press stuffing into cavity, roll up meat and tie securely at intervals with string. Place roast, fat side up, on rack in a roasting pan; brush with extra marmalade. Insert meat thermometer in thickest muscle, not against bone or fat. Roast in a 325°F oven for 25–29 minutes per pound for rare (140°F) or 29–32 minutes per pound for medium (150–155°F). Let stand 15–20 minutes before carving.
3 Place roasting pan on stove top over a low heat. Add wine and stir well to incorporate any brown bits. Bring to a boil; reduce heat and simmer until reduced to a thin sauce. Stir in extra orange peel and extra marmalade.
4 Remove string from lamb. Slice thinly. Spoon sauce over lamb to serve.

Roast Shoulder of Lamb with Mustard and Red Currant Glaze

Preparation time:
 20 minutes
Cooking time:
 1½ hours
Serves 8–10

1 4-pound boneless lamb shoulder roast, rolled and tied
2 tablespoons Dijon mustard
¼ cup red currant jelly
1 clove garlic, crushed
2 teaspoons oil
2 teaspoons soy sauce

1 Trim excess fat from lamb. Combine mustard, jelly, garlic, oil and soy sauce. Brush glaze over lamb.
2 Place lamb on a rack in a shallow roasting pan. Roast in a 350°F oven for 1½ hours or until a meat thermometer registers 140°F for rare, 150–155°F for medium. Let stand for 15–20 minutes before carving.
3 Slice lamb and serve with rice and vegetables.

15

Indian-Style Lamb

Preparation time:
40 minutes plus
overnight marinating
Cooking time:
1½–2½ hours
Serves 8–10

1 5–7 pound leg of
*lamb, trimmed of all
fat*
Marinade
⅓ *cup almonds*
2 *medium onions,
chopped*
6–8 *cloves garlic, peeled*
2-*inch piece gingerroot,
peeled*
4 *fresh chili peppers,
chopped*
¼ *cup plain yogurt*
2 *tablespoons lemon
juice*
¼ *cup vegetable oil*
½ *teaspoon each ground
coriander, cumin,
cayenne pepper and
garam masala (see
hint)*
*freshly ground black
pepper*

1 Make deep slashes in
leg of lamb with a
small, sharp knife. Place
leg of lamb in a baking
dish. Set aside.
2 To prepare Marinade:
Place almonds, onions,
garlic, gingerroot, chili
peppers and yogurt in a
food processor or
blender. Process until a
paste is formed. Paste
will be thick.
3 Transfer to a bowl.

Stir in remaining
ingredients. Spoon
marinade over lamb,
pushing some into
slashes in meat.
4 Turn leg over to
ensure that entire leg is
covered thickly with
marinade. Cover with
plastic wrap. Marinate
in refrigerator for at
least 24 hours, turning
occasionally.
5 Remove plastic wrap.
Roast in a 325°F oven
for 17–20 minutes per
pound for rare (140°F)
or 21–24 minutes per
pound for medium
(150–155°F). Let stand
15–20 minutes before
carving.
6 If desired, garnish
meat with whole toasted
almonds.

Note: Roast the lamb in
a glass or ceramic
baking dish rather than
a metal ovenproof dish
so as not to affect the
flavor of the marinade.

HINT

Garam masala is a
seasoning blend from
the cuisine of
Northern India. You
can purchase it at
Asian markets or mix
the ground spices of
pepper, cumin,
coriander, cardamom
and cinnamon.

Indian-Style Lamb

Rack of Lamb with Tropical Seasoning

Rack of Lamb with Tropical Seasoning

Preparation time:
  50 minutes
Cooking time:
  ¾–1¼ hours
Serves 4

2 racks of lamb, each
  with 6 cutlets (also
  called double French
  rack)
½ cup mint jelly
2 tablespoons pineapple
  juice
Tropical Seasoning
2 tablespoons butter
1 cup fresh bread crumbs
1 cup crushed pineapple
¼ cup pineapple juice
2 tablespoons finely
  chopped fresh mint
1 teaspoon grated
  gingerroot
Red Currant Mint Sauce
1 tablespoon red
  currant jelly
1 tablespoon hot water
2 tablespoons red wine
  vinegar
2 tablespoons finely
  chopped fresh mint

1 Trim excess fat from
lamb. Combine mint
jelly and pineapple juice.
Place racks fat side up
on a rack in a shallow
roasting pan. Brush with
some of the mint jelly
mixture. Roast in 375°F
oven until a meat
thermometer registers
140°F for rare,
150–155°F for medium.
Brush with remaining
mint jelly mixture.
Cover and let stand for
10–15 minutes before
slicing. Keep warm.
2 To prepare Tropical
Seasoning: Heat butter
in pan. Add bread
crumbs. Cook, stirring,
until golden. Stir in
pineapple, juice, mint
and gingerroot. Place in
a heatproof dish. Bake,
uncovered, in a 375°F
oven for 15 minutes or
until golden.
3 To prepare Red
Currant Mint Sauce:
Combine all ingredients
in a small saucepan.
Cook, stirring, until
warm. Slice racks of lamb
and serve with Tropical
Seasoning and sauce.

Note: Ask your butcher
to cut through the bones
for ease of slicing.

Crusty Leg of Lamb

Preparation time:
  30 minutes
Cooking time:
  1½–2 hours
Serves 8

1 7-pound leg of lamb
2 egg yolks, lightly
  beaten
¼ cup butter, melted
1 cup cornflake crumbs
1 tablespoon sesame
  seeds
½ teaspoon dried mixed
  herbs
1 small onion, sliced

1 Trim excess fat from
lamb. Brush top with a
little egg yolk.
2 Combine butter,
cornflake crumbs, sesame
seeds, mixed herbs and
half remaining egg yolk.
Press mixture firmly
over top of lamb.
Separate onion slices
into rings and arrange in
a pattern over the crumb
surface, pressing with
the palm of your hand.
Brush onion rings with
rest of egg yolk.
3 Place lamb on a rack
in a roasting pan. Roast
in a 325°F oven for
13–15 minutes per
pound for rare (140°F)
or 16–18 minutes per
pound for medium
(150–155°F). When the
crust becomes golden
and crisp, cover with
foil for the rest of the
cooking time.
4 Serve with mint sauce.

HINT
Roast meats on a rack
or trivet set in a
shallow roasting pan.
This will keep the
meat away from the
drippings that fall into
the roasting pan as the
meat cooks. When
roasting meats, choose
tender cuts. Unlike
braising or stewing,
roasting will not
tenderize meat.

Rack of Lamb with Chive Crust

Preparation time:
30 minutes
Cooking time:
1–1¼ hours
Serves 6

½ cup fine dry bread
   crumbs
2 teaspoons chopped
   fresh chives
2 teaspoons chopped
   mint
1 clove garlic, crushed
1 tablespoon lemon juice
1 teaspoon finely
   shredded lemon peel
2 racks of lamb, each
   with 6 cutlets, trimmed
¼ cup butter, melted
Sauce
¼ cup white wine
¼ cup water
1 teaspoon brown sugar
1 tablespoon lemon juice
⅓ cup butter, cubed
1 tablespoon mint jelly

1 Combine first six
ingredients in a small
bowl. Add water, 1
teaspoon at a time, if
mixture is too dry.
2 Press mixture firmly
over fatty side of racks.
Drizzle butter over crust.
3 Place lamb racks,
crust side up, in a
roasting pan. Roast in a
375°F oven for 25–27
minutes per pound for
rare (140°F) or 28–30
minutes per pound for
medium (150–155°F).
4 Let meat stand for 15
minutes before slicing.
Drain off all except 2
tablespoons of juice.
5 To prepare Sauce:
Place roasting pan on
top of stove and stir
wine and water into
juices. Bring to a boil,
stirring well. Boil until
reduced by half.
6 Stir in sugar and
lemon juice. Whisk in
butter one cube at a
time. Blend in mint jelly.
Serve with lamb.

HINT

Technically, lamb is a
young sheep no more
than a year old; at
two years it becomes
mutton. There is a
tendency to refer to
all meat of the sheep
as lamb. Both lamb
and mutton are
equally delicious,
lamb being very
tender and mutton
having a richer flavor
but requiring longer,
slower cooking.

HINT

Spring is the prime
time for tender young
lamb. Enjoy this
succulent favorite
while in season.

Rack of Lamb with Chive Crust

Roast Leg of Lamb with Red Currant Sauce

Preparation time:
  30 minutes
Cooking time:
  1¾–2¼ hours
Serves 6

2 leeks, sliced
¼ cup golden raisins
¼ cup packaged stuffing
  mix
2 tablespoons pine nuts
1 tablespoon tomato
  sauce
1 egg, beaten
1 7-pound leg of lamb,
  boned
freshly ground black
  pepper to taste
¼ cup water
½ cup chicken stock
1 tablespoon brandy
1 tablespoon red
  currant jelly
1 tablespoon cornstarch

1 Combine leeks, raisins, stuffing mix, pine nuts, tomato sauce and egg. Mix well. Spoon mixture into opening in leg. Join opening with skewers and secure with string, if necessary.
2 Slash fat on top side of leg with a sharp knife in a criss-cross pattern. Rub with pepper. Place meat, fat side up, on a rack in a roasting pan. Roast in a 325°F oven for 25–29 minutes per pound for rare (140°F) or 29–32 minutes per pound for medium (150–155°F).
3 Let lamb stand 15–20 minutes before carving. Strain cooking liquid into a bowl. Return to roasting pan with stock, brandy and jelly.
4 Blend cornstarch with a little of the liquid to form a smooth paste. Stir into sauce. Heat, stirring constantly, until sauce boils and thickens. Reduce heat and simmer for 3 minutes. Serve roast with sauce and vegetables of choice.

Note: Ask your butcher to 'tunnel bone' the leg for you.

HINT
There is a variety of packaged stuffing mixes on the market. You can vary the flavor by adding other ingredients such as fresh herbs, spices and citrus peel.

Roast Leg of Lamb with Garlic and Rosemary

Preparation time:
  20 minutes
Cooking time
  1½–2¼ hours
Serves 6–8

1 7–9 pound leg of lamb
2 cloves garlic
fresh rosemary sprigs
1 tablespoon oil
freshly ground black
  pepper
Mint Sauce, see page 61

1 Trim excess fat from lamb. Cut garlic cloves into thin slivers. Using a

Roast Leg of Lamb with Garlic and Rosemary

small sharp knife cut small slits over lamb. Insert garlic and rosemary sprigs into slits.

2 Brush lamb with oil and sprinkle with black pepper. Place lamb on a rack in a roasting pan. Roast in a 325°F oven for 13–15 minutes per pound for rare (140°F) or 16–18 minutes per pound for medium (150–155°F). Let stand 15–20 minutes before carving.

3 Serve lamb with Mint Sauce and seasonal vegetables.

HINT
Fresh rosemary is best for this recipe. If using dried rosemary, chop finely and rub into the slits in the lamb.

Heartland Crown Roast of Pork

*F*resh pork has a new and improved nutrition profile: it's leaner than ever before and lower in calories and cholesterol. The pork industry has responded to public demand for more healthful pork by producing leaner products that meet consumers' nutritional needs. And the variety of those cuts makes meal planning a snap for busy consumers.

This leaner low-fat pork does not need a long cooking time, which makes meat stringy and dry. Using a meat thermometer, cook pork to an internal temperature of 160°F (remove meat at 155°F and it will rise to 160°F while standing 10–15 minutes before carving).

Heartland Crown Roast of Pork

Preparation time:
  20 minutes
Cooking time:
  1½ hours
Serves 16

🍳 🍳

1 8–9 pound crown roast of pork
1 pound ground pork, cooked and drained
5 cups dry bread cubes
1 14½-ounce can chicken broth
½ cup chopped onion
½ cup chopped celery
1 cup walnut halves, toasted
1 teaspoon salt
¼ teaspoon ground cinnamon
¼ teaspoon ground allspice
⅛ teaspoon pepper
2 cups sliced fresh or frozen rhubarb, thawed
½ cup sugar

1 Place roast in a shallow roasting pan. Roast in a 350°F oven for 1½ hours or until meat thermometer registers 155°F. Remove roast from oven. Let stand 10 minutes before carving.

2 For stuffing, combine cooked ground pork, bread cubes, chicken broth, onion, celery, walnuts, salt, cinnamon, allspice and pepper. Mix well.
3 In a saucepan combine rhubarb and sugar. Bring to a boil. Pour over bread mixture and mix lightly.
4 Spoon stuffing into a buttered 2-quart casserole. Cover and bake alongside pork in a 350°F oven for 1½ hours.
5 To serve, line inside of roast with blanched broccoli flowerets. Spoon cooked stuffing into center. Garnish platter with fresh fruit, if desired.

HINT

To use a meat thermometer, insert thermometer into the center of the largest muscle or thickest portion of meat. The thermometer should not touch any fat or bone or the bottom of the roasting pan. When the meat reaches the desired temperature, push the thermometer into the meat a little farther. If the temperature drops, continue cooking. If the temperature stays the same, remove roast from oven. The meat will continue to cook slightly when removed from the oven. If you like, remove the roast when the thermometer registers 5 degrees below the desired doneness.

Pork Tenderloin with Apple and Mustard Sauce

Preparation time:
  30 minutes
Cooking time:
  20–30 minutes
Serves 4

1½ *pounds pork*
  tenderloin
1 *tablespoon butter*
1 *tablespoon oil*
Sauce
1 *clove garlic, crushed*
½ *teaspoon grated*
  gingerroot
1 *tablespoon seeded*
  mustard
¼ *cup applesauce*
¼ *cup chicken stock*
½ *cup heavy cream*
1 *teaspoon cornstarch*

1 Trim the pork of excess fat. Tie the pork with string at 1-inch intervals to keep a good shape, if necessary.
2 Heat butter and oil in a large skillet over medium-high heat. Add the pork and cook until lightly browned all over. Remove and place pork on a rack in a roasting pan. (Reserve the cooking juices in skillet.) Roast in a 450°F oven for 20–30 minutes or until meat thermometer registers 155°F or center is slightly pink. Let stand 10 minutes before slicing; keep warm.
3 To prepare Sauce:
Reheat reserved cooking juices in skillet. Add garlic and gingerroot; cook and stir for 1 minute. Stir in mustard, applesauce and stock. Slowly stir in combined cream and cornstarch and stir constantly until mixture boils and thickens.
4 Slice pork and serve with sauce, roasted potatoes and steamed broccoli.

HINT
Pork tenderloin is the section of meat that runs under the middle loin.
Fillets can be thick fat pieces or they can be long skinny pieces, so the cooking time can vary because of this.

Pork Tenderloin with Apple and Mustard Sauce

27

Pork Loin with Maple Glaze

Preparation time:
  30 minutes
Cooking time
  45 minutes–1½ hours
Serves 6

1 2-pound rolled and
  tied double pork loin
  roast
2 tablespoons butter
2 tablespoons finely
  chopped chives
2 teaspoons ground
  coriander
½ teaspoon ground
  black pepper
⅓ cup maple syrup
⅓ cup brown sugar
2 tablespoons butter,
  melted
1 tablespoon seeded
  mustard

1 Trim excess fat from loin. Untie meat and open loin out; spread with butter and sprinkle with chives. Roll up loin and secure with string, tying neatly at intervals. Sprinkle evenly with combined coriander and pepper.
2 Combine maple syrup, brown sugar, butter and mustard. Place pork on a rack in a roasting pan.
3 Roast pork in a 325°F oven for 45 minutes–1½ hours or until meat thermometer registers 155°F. Baste frequently with maple syrup mixture during the last 20 minutes of roasting. Remove from oven and brush with any remaining maple syrup mixture. Cover meat with foil and let stand 10 minutes before carving.
4 Slice pork and serve with Piquant Plum Sauce (page 62) and desired vegetables.

Pork Loin with Maple Glaze

HINT
A boneless pork loin roast weighing 2–4 pounds is also called Chef's Prime. It's just the right size for today's small family.

and Piquant Plum Sauce

regular intervals. Rub combined spices evenly over pork.

2 Place onions over bottom of roasting pan. Place pork on top of onions and drizzle oil over pork. Roast, uncovered, in a 350°F oven for 1 hour.

3 Sprinkle pork with brown sugar and roast 15–30 minutes more or until a meat thermometer registers 155°F. Let meat stand 15 minutes before carving. Keep warm. Serve pork with vegetables and a salad.

HINT

Fresh ham or pork leg is a lean and economical cut of pork. It can be roasted whole, as in the recipe for Spicy Leg of Pork, or it can be sliced or cubed for stir-fry or cut into cutlets and sauteed. If you can't find boneless leg of pork, ask your butcher to bone it for you. Or, substitute a boneless single loin pork roast.

Spicy Leg of Pork

Preparation time:
  30 minutes
Cooking time:
  1½ hours
Serves 16

1 4-pound boneless
  fresh ham (pork leg)

2 teaspoons ground cumin
2 teaspoons ground
  cardamom
2 teaspoons ground
  ginger
3 large onions, sliced
1 tablespoon oil
2 tablespoons brown
  sugar

1 Trim excess fat from pork and score at

Pork Loin with Apple and Prune Stuffing

Pork Loin with Apple and Prune Stuffing

Preparation time:
40 minutes
Cooking time:
1–1½ hours
Serves 8

1 Granny Smith apple,
  peeled, cored and
  chopped
⅓ cup chopped pitted
  prunes
2 tablespoons port
1 3-pound rolled and tied
  double pork loin roast
Sauce
2 tablespoons port
¼ cup butter, cubed

1 Combine apple, prunes
and port in a small bowl.
Trim excess fat from loin.
Untie meat and open loin
out; spread with apple
mixture. Roll up loin
and secure with string,
tying neatly at intervals.
2 Place pork on a rack
in a roasting pan. Roast
in a 325°F oven for
1–1½ hours or until a
meat thermometer
registers 155°F.
3 Remove roast from
oven and cover with
foil. Let stand 10
minutes before carving.
4 Meanwhile, drain off
all except 2 tablespoons
of pan juices from
roasting pan. Heat on
top of the stove and add
port. Bring to a boil,
stirring constantly, until
liquid is reduced by half.
5 Whisk in butter one
piece at a time. Serve
pork with sauce and
cooked vegetables.

HINT
The cooking times for
all roasts are based
on minutes per pound
and are estimates
only. Cooking times
vary with individual
cuts and your
preferences.

Roast Butterflied Pork

Preparation time
50 minutes plus
overnight marinating
Cooking time:
2 hours
Serves 16

1 6-pound fresh ham
  (leg of pork)
2 cloves garlic, crushed
6 whole cloves
2 bay leaves
sprigs of fresh thyme
¼ cup oil
¼ cup lemon juice
½ cup red wine

1 Using a sharp knife
start at the thick end of
the pork leg and cut
down and around pork
bone. Working carefully,
scrape away as much
meat from the bone as
you can; remove bone.
Cut down through the
thickest part of the
meat, but not right to
the bottom, so that pork
can be opened out flat.
2 Make several slits ¼
inch deep all over pork.
Fill with crushed garlic
and cloves. Place pork in
a flat glass dish and add
bay leaves and thyme.
Pour over oil, lemon
juice and red wine, cover
and marinate overnight.
3 Remove pork from
marinade; reserve
marinade. Roll up pork
and place on a rack in a
roasting pan. Roast for
1½ hours or until meat
thermometer registers
155°F, basting frequently
with reserved marinade.
Let stand for 15 minutes
before carving. Slice
pork and serve with
Applesauce (page 61).

HINT
When buying pork
look for flesh that is
light pink with
creamy white fat; this
indicates a tender cut.

POULTRY AND GAME

Roast Chicken with Tarragon and Bacon

*R*oast poultry is flavorful, easy and nutritious. *When handling poultry, it is important to keep these safety tips in mind. Always rinse fresh raw poultry with cold water and pat dry with paper towels. Refrigerate raw poultry and use within two days. Always defrost frozen poultry in the refrigerator or microwave oven; never let poultry stand at room temperature to thaw as bacteria will multiply rapidly. Always cook poultry to well-done. When poultry is properly cooked, it is no longer pink and the juices will be clear. Always wash hands, countertops and utensils in hot soapy water between each step of food preparation. Never leave food out at room temperature for more than 2 hours. Always thoroughly reheat leftovers before eating.*

Chicken and turkey lend themselves to fruit-filled stuffings, blended with garlic, spices, nuts and bread crumbs. Use fresh herbs liberally; try fresh mint, parsley, cilantro and tarragon. Marinades and glazes flavor and tenderize chicken. For a flavor variation when roasting poultry, place a layer of carrot and celery sticks in the roasting pan—this also makes a tasty gravy.

When roasting geese and ducks, prick the skin across the breast and thigh area with a fine skewer. This releases excess fat from the bird. Baste well during cooking to keep bird moist.

Quails should be roasted until just tender; overcooking produces tough dry meat. The more simply game birds are cooked the better.

Roast Chicken with Tarragon and Bacon

Preparation time:
  30 minutes
Cooking time:
  1½ hours
Serves 4

1 3-pound chicken
2 large sprigs fresh
   tarragon or rosemary
salt
pepper
3–5 slices bacon

1 tablespoon oil
½ cup chicken stock
2 teaspoons chopped
   fresh tarragon, extra

1 Remove excess fat from chicken. Rinse with cold water and pat dry with paper towels.

Place tarragon sprigs, salt and pepper in cavity of prepared chicken.
2 Lay bacon slices criss-cross over chicken breast, cutting slices to fit, if necessary. Secure bacon in several places with skewers or toothpicks.
3 Place chicken on a rack in a roasting pan; brush with oil. Roast in a 350°F oven about 1½ hours or until no longer pink, basting frequently with stock. (Cover chicken with foil, if necessary, to prevent overbrowning of bacon.) Let chicken stand 10 minutes before carving; keep warm.
4 Add extra tarragon to pan juices. Bring to a boil and pour over chicken before serving.

HINT
To defrost frozen birds health authorities strongly recommend thawing in the refrigerator as poultry is particularly susceptible to bacterial growth at room temperature. Take the poultry out of the freezer but don't unwrap it, because the skin tends to dry and toughen when exposed to air. Thaw completely in the refrigerator; this can take up to 24 hours for a 3-pound bird.

Traditional Roast Chicken with Mushroom Sauce

Preparation time:
 40 minutes
Cooking time:
 1½–1¾ hours
Serves 4

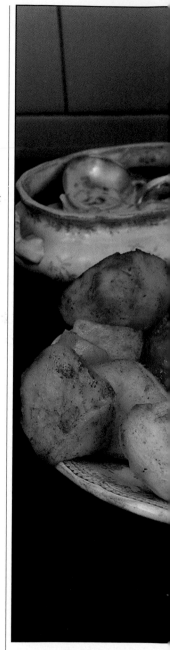

1 3-pound chicken
Stuffing
2 cups fresh bread
  crumbs
1 onion, finely chopped
4 ounces mushrooms,
  finely chopped
1 stalk celery, finely
  chopped
1 tablespoon chopped
  fresh parsley
1 teaspoon dried mixed
  herbs
freshly ground black
  pepper
1 egg, lightly beaten
Sauce
2 tablespoons butter
8 ounces mushrooms,
  sliced
4 shallots, chopped
2 tablespoons butter,
  extra
1 tablespoon all-purpose
  flour
¼ cup dry white wine
1 tablespoon dry sherry
¾ cup light cream
pinch white pepper

1 Remove excess fat from chicken. Rinse with cold water and pat dry with paper towels. Set aside.
2 To prepare Stuffing: Combine all ingredients for stuffing in a large bowl. Mix well with hands. Spoon loosely into cavity of chicken. Join cavity together with a skewer.
3 Place chicken, breast side up, on a rack in a roasting pan. Roast in a 350°F oven 1½–1¾ hours or until no longer pink. Let stand 10 minutes before carving. Keep warm.
4 To prepare Sauce: Melt butter in a saucepan. Cook mushrooms and shallots for 2 to 3 minutes and then remove from pan.
5 Melt extra butter. Add flour. Stir well. Cook 1 minute. Remove from heat. Gradually blend in wine, sherry, cream and pepper.
6 Return to heat. Cook, stirring constantly, until sauce boils and thickens. Stir in mushroom mixture and simmer for 3 minutes. Serve chicken with sauce.

HINT
Store cooked poultry no more than 2–3 days in coldest part of refrigerator. Remove stuffing and store separately. Reheat stuffing in a 350°F oven for 30 minutes or until thoroughly heated through. Always refrigerate broth or gravy in separate containers.

Traditional Roast Chicken with Mushroom Sauce

HOW TO STUFF A CHICKEN

Rinse chicken and pat dry with paper towels. Do not stuff bird until just before cooking. Loosely fill the neck cavity and body cavity with stuffing. Pull the neck skin to the back of the bird and fasten with a skewer. Tie chicken legs securely to tail using kitchen string. Twist the wing tips under the back, if desired. Place any remaining stuffing in a baking dish and refrigerate; then place stuffing in oven alongside the chicken during the last 30 minutes of roasting.

Roast Chicken with Fruit Stuffing

Preparation time:
  40 minutes
Cooking time:
  1½–1¾ hours
Serves 6

1 3-pound chicken
2 tablespoons butter
1 onion, finely chopped
½ cup chopped prunes
½ cup chopped dried
  apricots
½ cup seedless grapes
2 Granny Smith apples,
  peeled and sliced
½ teaspoon ground
  cinnamon
1 teaspoon brown sugar

*freshly ground black
  pepper*
2 tablespoons butter, extra
1 tablespoon lemon juice

1 Remove excess fat from chicken. Rinse with cold water and pat dry with paper towels. Set aside.
2 Melt butter in medium saucepan. Add onion and cook, stirring, until soft. Add prunes, apricots, grapes and apples and cook over a low heat for about 2 minutes. Stir in cinnamon and brown sugar. Spoon stuffing loosely into cavity of prepared chicken. Tie legs to tail and twist wing tips under.
3 Rub extra butter over chicken and drizzle with lemon juice. Place chicken on a rack in a roasting pan. Roast in a 350°F oven 1½–1¾ hours or until no longer pink. (Cover chicken with foil if necessary to prevent overbrowning.) Let stand 10 minutes before carving. Serve chicken with pan juices and rice.

Roast Turkey with Cashew Nut Stuffing

Preparation time:
  50 minutes
Cooking time:
  2–2½ hours
Serves 8

1 6-pound turkey,
  roasting hen, or capon
¼ cup butter
1 large onion, chopped
4 cups cooked brown
  rice
2 cups chopped dried
  apricots
1 cup unsalted cashew
  nuts
½ cup finely chopped
  parsley
⅓ cup finely chopped
  mint
2 tablespoons lemon
  juice
2 tablespoons oil
½ cup chicken stock

Roast Turkey with Cashew Nut Stuffing

Wine Gravy
¼ *cup all-purpose flour*
1½ *cups chicken stock*
½ *cup white wine*

1 Remove neck and giblets from inside turkey. Rinse turkey with cold water and pat dry with paper towels. Set aside.
2 Heat butter in a small pan. Add onion; cook until tender. Combine butter and onion with rice, apricots, cashews, parsley, mint and lemon juice; mix thoroughly.
3 Spoon stuffing loosely into cavity of turkey. Tie legs to tail with string. Tuck wings under turkey. Place turkey, breast side up, on rack in roasting pan. Rub oil over turkey. Roast in a 350°F oven for 2–2½ hours or until no longer pink and meat thermometer registers 180–185°F. Baste frequently with chicken stock. Loosely cover breast and legs with foil after 1 hour so skin does not darken too much. Let stand 20 minutes before carving. Keep warm. Serve with Wine Gravy.
4 To make Wine Gravy: Drain off all except 2 tablespoons of fat from roasting pan. Place pan over a low heat. Add flour. Stir well to incorporate all the brown bits. Cook, stirring constantly, over medium heat until well browned, taking care not to burn. Combine stock and wine. Gradually stir into flour mixture. Heat, stirring constantly until gravy boils and thickens.

37

HOW TO CARVE A TURKEY

A little practise and a sharp carving knife will soon have you carving confidently.

1 Cut into the bird where the ball joint of the wing meets the breast, and loosen the meat.

2 Continue cutting around the wing until the wing can be separated from the turkey body.

3 Tilt bird for a clear view of the angle of natural separation between the breast and thigh. Starting at the top, cut down through skin and meat to hip joint.

STEP-BY-STEP INSTRUCTIONS

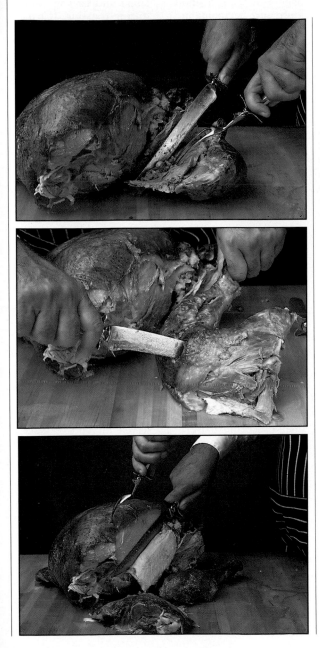

4 Continue cutting through the hip socket until the thigh and leg section can be loosened and removed from the body. Place section on carving board.

5 Separate thigh from leg by cutting through joint between. Cut meat from thigh into long, thin slices. Serve legs whole or sliced, according to size.

6 The breast is now ready to be carved. Start at the top of the breast, carving at an angle into thin slices. Repeat all steps to carve remaining side.

Turkey Breast with Apricot and Prune Stuffing

Preparation time:
1½ hours
Cooking time:
2–3 hours
Serves 8

🍲 🍲 🍲

1 4- to 5-pound bone-in
   turkey breast (see note)
Stuffing
3 cups fresh white bread
   crumbs or cubes
1 cup chopped pitted
   prunes
1 cup chopped dried
   apricots
4 shallots, finely chopped
½ cup port or dry sherry
shredded peel of 1
   orange and 1 lemon
1 egg, lightly beaten
Baste
½ cup apricot nectar
   (from canned apricots,
   see Garnish)
1 tablespoon brown sugar
1 tablespoon teriyaki
   sauce
Sauce
½ cup dried apricots
½ cup water
1 cup water, extra
1 teaspoon instant chicken
   bouillon granules
2 tablespoons brandy
1 tablespoon cornstarch
freshly ground black
   pepper
Garnish
canned apricot halves in
   nectar (reserve nectar
   for basting)
prunes
fresh orange slices

1 To bone the breast (see page 42): Using a small knife and beginning at the narrow end, ease the meat away from the bone along each side. Follow the contours of the bones, scraping where necessary.
2 Cut around the joint of the wing and lengthwise towards the body of the bird to expose the bone. Cut through the ligaments at the joint. Remove bone.
3 Continue easing flesh off the rib-cage on both sides until the backbone is exposed. Cut along backbone to free meat.
4 To prepare Stuffing: In a bowl combine bread crumbs, prunes, apricots, shallots, port and orange and lemon peels. Mix until well combined and stir in beaten egg. Use hands to bind mixture. Spread stuffing down center of boned turkey. Roll up. Place any remaining stuffing in a small casserole. Cover and refrigerate.
5 Using a heavy duty needle and cotton thread, sew up turkey to seal breast. Tuck in the skin at the neck end and finish off securely.
6 Place turkey on a rack in a roasting pan. Bake in a 350°F oven for 2–3 hours or until no longer pink and a meat thermometer registers 170°F. Baste frequently with the combined

apricot nectar, brown sugar and teriyaki sauce during roasting. (Cover with foil if necessary to prevent overbrowning.) Place casserole with stuffing in oven alongside turkey during the last 30 minutes of roasting. Cover with foil and let stand 20 minutes before carving.
7 To make Apricot Sauce: Combine apricots and ½ cup water in a saucepan and bring to a boil. Reduce heat and simmer until tender. Process or blend apricots until smooth. Return to pan and add 1 cup water and bouillon. Stir together brandy and cornstarch; add to apricot mixture. Cook and stir until mixture boils and thickens. Season with freshly ground pepper.
8 To serve turkey, decorate with apricot halves, prunes and orange slices. Slice turkey and serve with Apricot Sauce.

Note: If using frozen turkey breast, allow plenty of time to thaw in the refrigerator. Allow 24 hours for every 5 pounds. For faster thawing, place poultry in its original wrapping in a sink or large bowl. Cover with cold water, changing water often. Allow 30 minutes for each pound. Never thaw poultry at room temperature.

Turkey Breast with Apricot and Prune Stuffing

STEP-BY-STEP INSTRUCTIONS

Boning and Stuffing a Turkey Breast

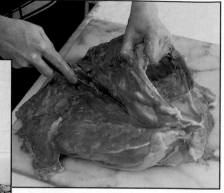

3 *Ease flesh off rib cage.*

1 *Ease meat away from bone along each side, following contours of bones.*

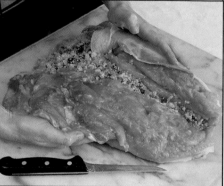

4 *Spread stuffing down center of turkey. Roll up.*

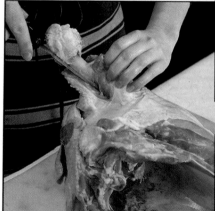

2 *Cut around joint of the wing and lengthwise towards the body of the bird.*

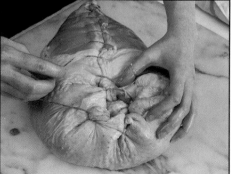

5 *Sew up breast. Tuck in skin at neck end.*

Oriental Chicken

Preparation time:
  20 minutes plus
overnight marinating
Cooking time:
  1¼–1½ hours
Serves 6

1 3-pound chicken
Marinade
¼ cup soy sauce
2 tablespoons teriyaki
  sauce
2 tablespoons honey
2 tablespoons dry sherry
2 tablespoons lemon juice
2 shallots, finely sliced
1 teaspoon grated
  gingerroot
¼ teaspoon five spice
  powder
¼ teaspoon sesame oil

Sauce
1 tablespoon cornstarch
1 cup water
1 teaspoon instant chicken
  bouillon granules

1 Rinse chicken with cold water and pat dry with paper towels. Place in a plastic bag.
2 Mix together all ingredients for marinade in a bowl. Pour over chicken in bag. Seal bag. Place on a plate. Marinate in the refrigerator overnight, turning occasionally.
3 Remove chicken from bag. Reserve marinade. Place chicken on a rack in a roasting pan. Roast in a 350°F oven for 1¼–1½ hours or until no longer pink. Baste frequently with marinade.
4 To prepare Sauce: Blend cornstarch with a little water. Combine with remaining water, marinade and bouillon in a small saucepan.
5 Heat, stirring constantly, until sauce boils and thickens. Simmer for 3 minutes. Serve chicken with sauce, rice and salad.

HINT

To store unused fresh gingerroot, peel, cut into thick slices, place in a screwtop jar and cover with dry sherry. Store in refrigerator.

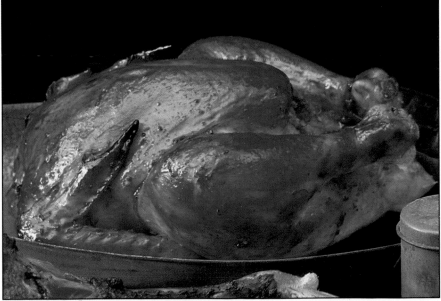

Oriental Chicken

HOW TO CARVE A DUCK

Follow these simple step-by-step instructions to cut and serve roast duck with skill and ease. You will need sharp poultry shears or kitchen scissors.

1 Let duck stand for about 15 minutes after roasting. Starting at tail opening, cut with poultry shears through breast and up to neck.

2 Turn bird over and cut with shears on one side of the backbone and separate into halves.

3 Follow the natural line between breast and thigh and cut crosswise into quarters. (Use this method to carve small game birds also.)

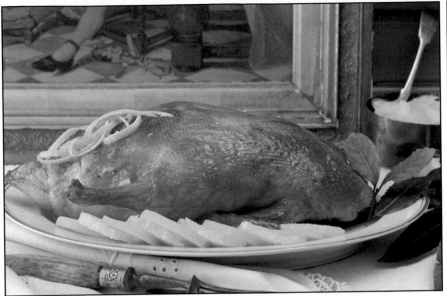

Duck with Orange Sauce

Duck with Orange Sauce

Preparation time:
  40 minutes
Cooking time:
  1¾–2¼ hours
Serves 6

1 4- to 5-pound
  domestic duckling
Stuffing
2 cups cooked rice
½ cup pine nuts
½ cup golden raisins
4 shallots, chopped
juice and shredded peel
  of 1 orange
1 clove garlic, crushed
freshly ground black
  pepper
Sauce
2 tablespoons all-
purpose flour
1 cup white wine
½ cup orange juice
freshly ground pepper
2 oranges, segmented

1 Remove all loose fat from the duck. Rinse with cold water and pat dry with paper towels. Set aside.
2 To prepare Stuffing: Combine all ingredients for stuffing. Mix well. Press loosely into the cavity of prepared duck. Tuck legs under the band of skin across the tail. Twist wing tips under back.
3 Place duck, breast side up, on a rack in a roasting pan. Prick skin well all over. Roast in a 375°F oven for 1¾–2½ hours or until meat thermometer registers 180–185°F. Remove fat from pan during roasting. Let stand 15 minutes.
4 To prepare Sauce: Remove all except 2 tablespoons of pan juices from pan. Heat on top of stove. Add flour and stir well. Cook 1 minute. Remove from heat; add wine and orange juice.
5 Return to the heat. Cook, stirring constantly, until sauce boils and thickens. Simmer for 3 minutes. Add pepper and orange segments.
6 Serve duck with sauce, stuffing and cooked vegetables.

Orange Garlic Duck

Preparation time:
  40 minutes
Cooking time:
  1¾–2½ hours
Serves 6

1 *4- to 5-pound*
  domestic duckling
1 *orange*

6 *cloves garlic, crushed*
2 *tablespoons butter*
freshly ground black
  pepper
2 *teaspoons all-purpose*
  flour
¾ *cup dry white wine*

1 Remove all loose fat from the duck. Rinse with cold water and pat dry with paper towels. Set aside.
2 Quarter orange.

Combine garlic, butter and pepper; mix well. Put garlic butter into cavity of duck and add quartered orange. Tuck legs under the band of skin across the tail. Twist wing tips under back.
3 Place duck, breast side up, on a rack in a roasting pan. Prick skin well all over. Roast in a 375°F oven for 1¾–2½ hours or until meat

Orange Garlic Duck

thermometer registers 180–185°F. Remove fat from pan during roasting. Let stand 15 minutes.

4 Drain all but 1 tablespoon of fat from roasting pan. Place pan over a low heat. Add flour. Stir well to incorporate all the brown bits. Cook, stirring constantly, over medium heat until well browned, taking care not to burn. Gradually stir in wine and any juices from duck. Heat, stirring constantly until sauce boils and thickens. Serve duck with roast potatoes and cooked vegetables.

HINT

Before cooking a whole duck, remove all the excess fat and press the oil glands near the base of the tail to empty them.

Roast Goose

Preparation time:
40 minutes
Cooking time:
2¾–3¼ hours
Serves 10

1 8- to 10-pound domestic goose
2 tablespoons butter
1 onion, finely chopped
2 Granny Smith apples, peeled and chopped
1½ cups chopped pitted prunes
3 cups small cubes of bread
2 teaspoons grated lemon peel
½ cup chopped parsley
1 tablespoon all-purpose flour
1 tablespoon all-purpose flour, extra
2 tablespoons brandy
1½ cups chicken stock

1 Remove all loose fat from goose. Rinse with cold water and pat dry with paper towels. Using a fine skewer, prick the skin across the breast area. Set aside.

2 Melt butter in a saucepan. Add onion and cook and stir until tender. Combine onion mixture with apples, prunes, bread, lemon and parsley; mix thoroughly. Spoon stuffing loosely into cavity of goose. Tuck legs under the band of skin across the tail. Twist wing tips under.

3 Sprinkle 1 tablespoon flour over goose. Place goose, breast side up, on a rack in a roasting pan. Roast in 350°F oven for 2¾–3¼ hours or until a meat thermometer registers 180–185°F. Remove fat from pan during roasting. Remove from roasting pan and let stand 15 minutes before carving.

4 Drain all but 1 tablespoon fat from roasting pan and place over a low heat. Add extra flour and stir well to incorporate all the brown bits. Cook, stirring constantly, over medium heat until well browned, taking care not to burn. Gradually stir in brandy and stock. Heat, stirring constantly, until sauce boils and thickens. Serve goose with gravy, roast potatoes and creamed onions.

HINT

During roasting time, baste goose with its own, plentiful fat. This melts out more fat and helps crisp the skin.

Roast Quails with Bacon and Rosemary

Roast Quails with Bacon and Rosemary

Preparation time:
 40 minutes
Cooking time:
 40–50 minutes
Serves 4

8 *quails*
1 *medium onion,
 chopped*
3 *slices bacon, chopped*
1 *tablespoon fresh
 rosemary leaves*
2 *tablespoons butter,
 melted*
½ *cup port*
¼ *cup water*
½ *cup light cream*
1 *teaspoon cornstarch*

1 Rinse quails with cold water and pat dry with paper towels. Tie the legs and wings of each bird close to its body with string.
2 Spread onion, bacon and rosemary over base of roasting pan and add quails. Brush each quail with melted butter. Pour ½ cup of combined port and water over quails.
3 Roast in a 375°F oven for 40–50 minutes or until the legs twist easily in their sockets. Let stand 10 minutes before serving; keep warm.
4 Carefully strain any juices from baking dish into a small pan; add remaining port and water mixture and bring to a boil. Reduce heat and gradually stir in combined cream and cornstarch, stirring until slightly thickened. Serve quail with sauce and cooked vegetables.

HINT
When eating quail it is quite correct to use fingers after eating the flesh from the breast with a knife and fork. Provide guests with finger bowls filled with warm water; add lemon slices or fragrant flowers for a special touch.

HINT
Tying the bird in a compact shape ensures even browning and cooking and makes handling the bird easier.

VEGETABLE ACCOMPANIMENTS

Parsnip and Zucchini with Ginger and Almonds, and Glazed Carrots

*F*resh seasonal vegetables make a perfect accompaniment to roast meats.

Vegetables should be prepared as simply as possible, cooked until just tender, dressed with herbs and seasoned lightly. Serve two or three fresh vegetables with roast meats to enhance and supplement the roast.

In this chapter we share with you our secret for the best roast potatoes, golden brown and crispy outside, moist and soft inside. We've also included favorites such as Sweet Nugget Pumpkins Julienne, Braised Onions in Cream, and Broccoli with Browned Nut Butter Sauce.

Parsnip and Zucchini with Ginger and Almonds

Preparation time:
  5 minutes
Cooking time:
  10 minutes
Serves 6

3 parsnips, peeled and
  sliced
3 zucchini, sliced
1 teaspoon finely
  chopped fresh
  gingerroot
1 tablespoon butter
2 tablespoons slivered
  almonds, toasted

Boil, steam or microwave parsnips and zucchini until tender. Add gingerroot, butter and toasted almonds; toss to combine. Serve immediately.

Glazed Carrots

Preparation time:
  15 minutes
Cooking time:
  15 minutes
Serves 6

8 medium carrots,
  peeled and sliced
¼ cup butter, melted
2 tablespoons brown
  sugar
1 tablespoon honey
chopped chives

1 Boil, steam or microwave carrots until tender.
2 Combine butter, brown sugar and honey; pour over carrots and toss. Serve immediately garnished with chopped chives.

Braised Onions in Cream

Preparation time:
  20 minutes
Cooking time:
  25 minutes
Serves 6

18 tiny white onions,
  peeled and trimmed
1 cup heavy cream
ground pepper

1 Place onions snugly in a single layer in shallow ovenproof dish.
2 In saucepan, heat cream until simmering; pour over onions. Season to taste with pepper.
3 Cover and bake in a 350°F oven for 15 minutes. Remove cover; continue baking until onions are tender, about 5–10 minutes more.

HINT
Use sweet pickling onions for this recipe. For ease of peeling top and tail onions, taking care to keep ends intact so that onions do not fall apart. Cover with boiling water for about 5 minutes to loosen their skins, drain and peel immediately.

Left: Baby Vegetables with Herbs

Baby Vegetables with Herbs

Preparation time:
  15 minutes
Cooking time:
  10 minutes
Serves 6–8

2 pounds seasonal baby
  vegetables
2 onions, chopped
¼ cup butter
¼ cup chopped parsley
¼ cup chopped fresh
  oregano or thyme
  (or 2 teaspoons dried)
ground pepper

1 Trim vegetables and wash. If large, cut into even-sized pieces.
2 In large saucepan, cook onions in butter over medium heat for 1 minute. Add vegetables and toss well to coat.
3 Cover vegetables; reduce heat and steam until all vegetables are crisp-tender, about 10 minutes.
4 Add parsley, herbs and pepper to taste.
Note: Choose from baby eggplant, carrots, baby squash (yellow or green), tiny onions, small green beans and zucchini; if using snow peas, add these near the end of Step 3 to avoid over-cooking.

HINT
When choosing vegetables, always demand freshness. If you buy in season you get the freshest vegetables at the best price. Do not buy vegetables in sealed plastic-wrapped packs because they will sweat and spoil. Buy only what you need or can store without waste.

Right: Sweet Nugget Pumpkins Julienne

Sweet Nugget Pumpkins Julienne

Preparation time:
  30 minutes
Cooking time:
  45 minutes
Serves 8

4 *small golden nugget*
  pumpkins
2 *tablespoons butter*
freshly ground black
  pepper
4 *medium carrots*
6 *ounces sweet*
  potatoes
⅔ *cup water*
2 *tablespoons honey*
chopped parsley

1 Halve pumpkins and scoop out seeds. Place, cut side up, in baking dish. Dot each with ½ teaspoon of the butter; sprinkle with pepper.
2 Bake in a 350°F oven until pumpkins are tender, about 45 minutes. Drain excess juice from halves.
3 When pumpkins are almost cooked, peel and cut carrots and sweet potatoes into short julienne sticks. Place in a saucepan with the water and honey.
4 Cover and bring to a boil; reduce heat and gently simmer until tender, about 8 to 10 minutes. Drain well.

5 Spoon carrot and sweet potato sticks into pumpkins. Garnish with parsley.

HINT
If golden nugget pumpkins are not available, substitute 1 medium butternut squash or 4 small acorn squash. Scoop out seeds and flesh leaving a 1-inch shell. Cook as directed.

Roast Potatoes

Preparation time:
15 minutes
Cooking time:
1½ hours
Serves 6

8 *medium russet*
potatoes, peeled
4 *ounces beef dripping*
or lard or ½ *cup oil*

1 Cut any large potatoes in half. Wash and dry.
2 Melt the beef dripping in a roasting pan in a 350°F oven. Add the potatoes. Turn them in the fat to ensure they are thoroughly coated. Roast in the upper half of the oven for 30 minutes, turning once.
3 Drain off all the fat from the potatoes. Continue to roast for 1 hour, turning once or twice, until cooked, crisp and golden.

HINT

☐ Roast potatoes are always crisper and more golden if cooked in a separate metal roasting pan.
☐ For quicker cooking, boil potatoes for 10 minutes, draining well, before adding to the fat.

Roast Potatoes, Peppers and Onions

Preparation time:
30 minutes
Cooking time:
45 minutes
Serves 6

6 *medium baking*
potatoes, peeled and
quartered lengthwise
1 *large red bell pepper,*
seeded and cut into 8
wedges
1 *large green bell*
pepper, seeded and cut
into 8 wedges
4 *onions, quartered*
lengthwise
4 *cloves garlic, finely*
chopped
3 *tablespoons olive oil*
1 *teaspoon dried*
rosemary
freshly ground black
pepper

1 Arrange potatoes and peppers alternately in a spoke pattern in a large, shallow, ovenproof dish.
2 Pile onions in the center. Scatter garlic over the top. Drizzle with oil and sprinkle with rosemary and pepper.
3 Bake in a 400°F oven for 45 minutes or until vegetables are lightly golden, crisp and tender.

Broccoli with Browned Nut Butter Sauce

Preparation time:
10 minutes
Cooking time:
15 minutes
Serves 6

Roast Potatoes, Peppers and Onions

12 stalks fresh broccoli
⅓ cup butter
¼ cup slivered or sliced
  almonds
squeeze of lemon juice
freshly ground black
  pepper

1 Steam broccoli over simmering water, covered, until tender (about 8 minutes). Drain and arrange on heated serving platter; keep warm.
2 Meanwhile, in medium saucepan melt butter over medium heat. Add almonds and cook until both nuts and butter are browned. (Careful—don't let the butter burn!)
3 Add a squeeze of lemon juice; pour over broccoli. Season to taste with pepper.

TRADITIONAL ACCOMPANIMENTS AND SAUCES

Apricot and Herb Stuffing

These traditional accompaniments are added extras that enhance roast meats. It certainly would be unfair on so splendid a dish as roast turkey to stint on sauces or stuffing and roast beef would not be half as grand without Yorkshire Pudding, a meaty gravy and horseradish sauce.

Accompaniments, sauces and stuffing help keep roast meats moist; they also provide contrasting color, flavor and texture. Most importantly, they turn everyday meats into special occasion meals.

Apricot and Herb Stuffing

Preparation time:
30 minutes
Cooking time:
none
Makes 3 cups

1 cup chopped dried apricots
¾ cup golden raisins
1 onion, chopped
1 stalk celery, finely chopped
3 cups fresh bread crumbs
1 tablespoon finely chopped parsley
¼ teaspoon dried sage
¼ teaspoon dried rosemary
¼ teaspoon dried thyme
1 egg, beaten

1 Mix all ingredients together in a large bowl. Place in a freezer container or plastic bag. Seal and freeze.
2 To use: Thaw completely. Place in the cavity of the prepared turkey and seal cavity with a skewer. Roast turkey as directed.

Sage and Onion Stuffing

Preparation time:
30 minutes
Cooking time:
none
Makes 3 cups

2 tablespoons butter
1 large onion, finely chopped
2 slices bacon, chopped
1 tablespoon chopped fresh sage
2 teaspoons grated lemon peel
3 cups dry stuffing mix
1 egg, lightly beaten

1 Heat butter in saucepan. Add onion and bacon and cook, stirring, until soft. Combine onion and bacon with sage, lemon peel, stuffing mix and egg. Mix thoroughly. Seal and freeze until required.
2 To use: Thaw completely. Place in the cavity of the prepared bird and seal cavity with a skewer. Roast as directed.

Walnut and Ham Stuffing

Preparation time:
30 minutes
Cooking time:
none
Makes 3 cups

1 cup finely chopped ham
½ cup finely chopped walnuts
½ cup finely chopped mushrooms
2 cups fresh bread crumbs
¼ cup chopped parsley
1 egg, lightly beaten

1 Mix all ingredients together in a large bowl Place in a freezer container or plastic bag. Seal and freeze until required.
2 To use: Thaw completely. Place in the cavity of the prepared bird and seal cavity with a skewer.

HINT
Butter a slice of day-old bread, rub with crushed garlic and place bread at the opening of the body cavity after stuffing a bird. The slice of bread acts as a lid and keeps stuffing from falling out.

1 Make a well in center of flour and salt mixture; drop in eggs.

2 Stir in milk to make a smooth batter.

3 Carefully fill each muffin cup two-thirds full with batter.

Yorkshire Puddings

Preparation time:
  15 minutes plus 1 hour standing
Cooking time:
  20 minutes
Makes 8

1 cup all-purpose flour
pinch salt
2 eggs
1 cup milk
1 tablespoon water
3 tablespoons lard, beef dripping or butter, melted

1 Stir together flour and salt in a large bowl. Make a well in the center. Drop in the eggs. Gradually beat in some of the milk to make a stiff but smooth batter, making sure there are no lumps. Gradually beat in the remaining milk. Strain into a jug. Cover and refrigerate for 1 hour. Stir in the water.
2 Spoon ¼ teaspoon of the fat into the base of each of 12 deep metal muffin pans or popover pans. Place in a 425°F oven for 3 to 5 minutes to heat the fat. Carefully fill each muffin pan two-thirds full with batter.
3 Bake in a 425°F oven for 15–20 minutes or until risen, golden and crisp. Serve at once.

HINT
□ Yorkshire puddings batter can be baked in an 8-inch round or square baking pan (increase time slightly).
□ For a lighter batter, use skim milk or ⅔ cup milk and ⅓ cup ice water.
□ 1 tablespoon of chopped fresh herbs or dried thyme to taste could be added to the batter.

Yorkshire Puddings

Game Chips

Preparation time:
 20 minutes plus 1 hour
 standing
Cooking time:
 15 minutes
Serves 4

1 pound potatoes
oil for deep-frying

1 Peel and slice potatoes
very thinly. Soak
potatoes in cold water
for 1 hour. Drain and
dry thoroughly on paper
towels.
2 Heat oil for deep-
frying in a heavy-based
saucepan. Fry potatoes
in small batches until
light golden brown.
Drain on paper towels.
3 To serve, fry potatoes
again until crisp. Drain
and serve immediately
with roast turkey or
goose.

HINT
Substitute sweet
potatoes for regular
potatoes in this
recipe, if desired.

Bread Sauce

Preparation time:
  15 minutes
Cooking time:
  5 minutes
Serves 4

1 small onion, finely
  chopped
1 cup milk
1 bay leaf
4 peppercorns
1 cup soft fresh white
  bread crumbs
1 tablespoon butter

Place onion, milk, bay
leaf and peppercorns in
a small saucepan and
simmer for 20 minutes.
Strain and then stir in
bread crumbs and butter.
Serve immediately.

HINT
Bread sauce is a
traditional
accompaniment to
roast turkey, goose or
chicken. Freshly
grated nutmeg and
ground cloves also
add flavor to this
traditional favorite.

Cumberland Sauce

Preparation time:
  15 minutes
Cooking time:
  10 minutes
Makes 2 cups

1 orange
1 lemon
1 cup red currant jelly
2 tablespoons Dijon
  mustard
¼ cup port
freshly ground black
  pepper

1 Remove peel from
orange and lemon and
cut into fine strips.
Cover with water,
simmer over low heat
for 5 minutes and drain.
2 Combine juice from
orange and lemon, red
currant jelly and
mustard in a small
saucepan. Heat gently,
stirring until jelly has
melted. Add port and
simmer for 3 minutes.
3 Season with pepper
and add orange and
lemon peel to serve.

Back left: Bread Sauce, Right: Cumberland Sauce

Mint Sauce

Preparation time:
  10 minutes
Cooking time:
  10 minutes
Makes 1 cup

¼ *cup water*
¼ *cup sugar*

⅓ *cup vinegar*
¼ *cup finely chopped
  mint*

Combine water and sugar in small saucepan. Bring to a boil, stirring until sugar is dissolved. Add vinegar and bring to a boil again. Remove from heat and stir in mint. Cool. Stir well before serving. Serve with roast lamb.

HINT
Chop mint just before adding to sauce to prevent discoloration.

Applesauce

Preparation time:
  20 minutes
Cooking time:
  30 minutes
Makes 2 cups

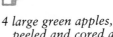

4 *large green apples,
  peeled and cored and
  chopped*
2 *tablespoons butter*
¼ *cup sugar*
2 *teaspoons grated
  lemon peel*
¼ *cup water*

Place apples, butter, sugar, lemon peel and water in a heavy based saucepan. Cook over a low heat, stirring frequently until the apples are soft and pulpy. Serve warm with roast pork, roast duck or goose.

HINT
Applesauce may be made up to 3 days in advance and stored covered in the refrigerator.

Front left: Applesauce, Right: Mint Sauce

Piquant Plum Sauce

Preparation time:
 20 minutes
Cooking time:
 30 minutes
Makes 2 cups

1 large onion, chopped
2 cloves garlic, crushed
1 tablespoon vegetable
 oil
1 30-ounce can unpitted
 purple plums, drained
 and pitted
½ cup water
⅓ cup lightly packed
 brown sugar
2 tablespoons white
 vinegar
2 teaspoons grated fresh
 gingerroot
½ teaspoon mustard
1 small red chili pepper,
 finely chopped

1 In large saucepan,
cook onion and garlic in
oil for 3 minutes. Add
plums, water, brown
sugar, vinegar,
gingerroot, mustard and
chili pepper; heat until
boiling.

2 Reduce heat; simmer,
uncovered, stirring
occasionally, until plums
are softened and sauce is
thick—about 15
minutes. (If sauce
becomes too thick, thin
with a little water.) Serve
warm with roast pork.

HINT
Use an equal
quantity of fresh
purple plums
when in season.

Piquant Plum Sauce